Brian Lara

Peter Leigh

Published in association with The Basic Skills Agency

Hodder & Stoughton

A MEMBER OF THE HODDER HEADLINE GROUP

Acknowledgements

Photos: p. 22 Action Images, pp. 3, 6 and 14 © Gordon Brooks, p. 20 Colorsport, pp. 8, 18, 24 and 28 © Patrick Eagar

Cover photo: © Patrick Eagar

A CIP record is available from the British Library

ISBN 0340 701080

First published 1997
Impression number 10 9 8 7 6 5 4 3 2 1
Year 2002 2001 2000 1999 1998 1997

Typeset by Fakenham Photosetting Ltd, Fakenham, Norfolk.
Printed in Great Britain for Hodder & Stoughton Educational, a division of Hodder Headline Plc, 338 Euston Road, London NW1 3BH by Page Bros Ltd, Norwich.

Contents

1 The records

The time is 11.46 a.m.

The date is Monday April 18, 1994.

The place is Antigua, in the West Indies.

The scene is the fifth Test Match
between England and the West Indies.
A young West Indian is batting.
The eyes of all the crowd are on him.

The people are quiet,
hardly daring to breathe.
It is hot,
and getting hotter.
People should be inside,
out of the sun.

But nobody moves.
No-one wants to miss this.

Outside the ground,
everyone has stopped what they are doing,
and is looking at the television.
It seems as if the whole world is watching
the young batsman.
The match is over.
The West Indies are going to win.
That's certain.
That's not why everyone is watching
the young batsman.

They are watching to see
if he is going to make history.

The English bowler runs up.
He knows why everyone is watching.
He puts everything into it,
and hurls the ball at the wicket.

The bat flashes down,
the ball is cracked to the boundary,
and the crowd goes wild!

He has done it!

Antigua, April 18 1994, Brian making cricketing history.

The young batsman was Brian Lara,
and he had just made 369,
the highest score of any batsman,
in any Test Match,
in any country ever!

He had just broken
one of the oldest records in cricket.

The crowd clapped and cheered,
and the English team gathered round
to shake Brian's hand.
Hundreds of people ran onto the pitch.
There was singing and dancing
all over the ground.

Then the police cleared a way
through the crowd,
and an old, white-haired man
began to make his way to the centre.

The crowd moved back to let him through.
They all knew him.
Slowly he walked up to Brian,
smiled, and shook him by the hand.

It was Sir Garfield Sobers,
one of the most famous cricketers
in the world,
and the man whose record
Brian had just broken.

Cricketers honour Brian after making the highest score of any batsman in a Test Match.

After the singing and dancing was over,
and the crowds
had gone back to their seats,
Brian went on to make 375
before he was finally out.

That is still the record for any batsman
in any Test Match.
But that wasn't the only record
that Brian Lara broke.

Straight after that match
he came to England
to play for Warwickshire.
In his fifth match for them he scored 501.
That is the highest score ever made
by any batsman,
in any match,
in any country!

Brian Lara was now the greatest batsman
the world had ever seen.

Brian celebrates his record-breaking score of 501 which he made for Warwickshire in 1994.

2 Trinidad

Brian Lara was born in 1969 in Trinidad.
He started playing cricket at the age of six.
He played every day for as long as he could.
And when he was not playing cricket,
he was practising cricket.

But he did not practise with a bat and a ball.
He practised with a broom handle
and a marble!
He would hit the marble
against the garage wall,
and pretend he was playing for the West Indies.

If he missed the marble he was out.
He didn't often miss!

Now Brian still practises like this.
Before he goes out to bat,
he often bounces a marble up and down
on a ruler.
He can do it for hours.

If you think it sounds easy,
try it yourself!

When he was young
Brian also watched lots of cricket.
Then he spent hours at home,
copying what he had seen.

He studied all the great players,
and tried to make himself
exactly like them,
and do exactly what they did.

That was how he learnt all the strokes.

But he also copied the way they played,
and the way they stood.

He even got his mother to buy a special shirt.
It had long sleeves
that buttoned round the wrist.
Roy Fredericks, a great West Indian batsman,
wore shirts like this,
and Brian had to look exactly like him.

At school,
Brian played a type of cricket called 'Pass-out'.
In this game there is no wicket,
but you are out if you miss the ball.

Brian's teacher said,
'Brian would be in there all day.
He never missed the ball.'

After school Brian played cricket
in the street with his friends,
or in the yard,
or wherever they could find space.

In these games Brian learnt
the tricks of cricket,
the things you don't learn in the text books.

But Brian didn't just play cricket.
He also thought about it a lot.

When he became captain of his school team,
the team won lots of matches.
But it wasn't just because of Brian's batting.
He thought about each match.
He thought about the strength
and the weakness
of the other team.
And he thought about the strength
and the weakness
of his own team.
And then he thought of a plan
to win the match.

And it usually worked.

He also brought out the best
in the rest of the team.
He was always very calm,
and he never shouted at them.
They looked up to him,
and listened to what he said.

And he was always smiling!
You can still see that smile today.

Brian is famous for his winning smile. Here he is with Viv Richards.

Brian was born into a very poor family,
and he has ten brothers and sisters.
But they are still a very close family.

Brian's father helped him a lot.
He helped him to practise,
and he always went to every match.

After the match they would talk.
Brian's father would go over
the things Brian had done well,
and the things he had done badly.
And they would work out
how to put them right.

But Brian's father
always had great faith in Brian.
He told everybody
that Brian would do great things.
They were very close.

And then when he was 18,
just before he won his first cap
for the West Indies,
Brian's father died.

Brian was very upset,
but he is very quiet, and did not show it.

And then after he made his world record 375,
he dedicated the innings to his father.

'You see,' he said,
'my father really believed in me,
and always told me that one day
I was going to do just this.
He was the sort of father
that every young boy should have.'

3 Becoming famous

As Brian was growing up
people said he would do great things
in cricket,
and Brian soon began to show them
that they were right.

In 1989
he was made captain of Trinidad.
He was 20.
He was the youngest captain ever.

Soon he broke more records.
He made
the highest number of runs in a season,
and made the third highest score ever
against Australia.
Brian still thinks this is his best innings.

Brian batting for the West Indies.

But it wasn't until that famous 375
that the world knew
how good Brian Lara was.
It was on the television
and in the newspapers
in England, Australia and India.
And it was headlines even in countries
that don't play cricket.

A newscaster in America
announced the news on television,
and then had to say
that he had no idea what it meant.
He had never seen cricket in his life!

The Prime Minister of Trinidad
had a special reception for Brian.
Streets were named after him,
and he was presented with the Trinity Cross,
the highest honour in Trinidad.

Brian signing autographs.

4 England

In 1994, soon after the record,
Brian left the West Indies.
He came to England
to play for Warwickshire.
They were keen to have Brian play for them.

When he arrived,
he had just one day
before he played his first match.
He had had no practice, and very little sleep.
The television and the press
would not leave him alone.
He was very big news,
and everybody wanted to see the great Brian Lara.

There were huge crowds all keen to see him play.
All this was pressure on Brian.
So it would not have been surprising
if he failed in his first innings.

But he did not fail.
He scored 147 off 160 balls.
One sports reporter said,
'It was the finest innings I have ever seen.'

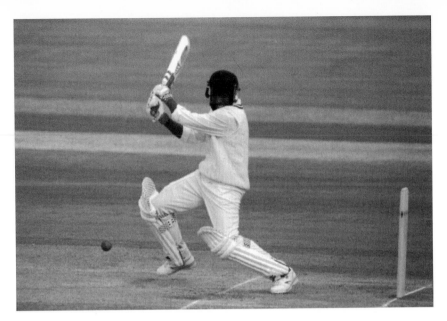

Brian playing his first match for Warwickshire in 1994.

Brian went on to destroy
every other team in England.
The best moment came
when he made his other famous,
record-breaking score
of 501 not out against Durham at Edgbaston in
1994.

After this many people said
that Brian wouldn't stay with Warwickshire.
They said that now he was a star,
he would quickly move on.
But Brian has stayed with Warwickshire.

They play in Birmingham.
'I like it here,' says Brian.
'The people have taken me to their hearts.'
Brian likes it so much,
he has helped Warwickshire
win every major trophy in English cricket.

Brian on his way to making 501 at Edgbaston in 1994.

He even likes English cricket!
He thinks the standard is high!
'The trouble is,' he says,
'the system over here doesn't help the players.
There are too many matches,
and they are too long.'

So what makes him so good?
Some say it is because he is so short.
Many great batsmen are short.
Some say it is the way he lifts his bat
before making the shot.
That gives him the grace and the power.
Others say it is the quickness of his eye.

Brian himself says,
'When another batsman faces the bowling,
he tries not to get out,
and, if he is lucky, score some runs.
When a West Indies batsman faces the bowling,
he tries to score a four off every ball!'

5 The future

When Brian was making all those great scores
people thought he would go on forever.
Brian was more realistic.
'There will be times,' he said,
'when I will fail.'

And he did fail in 1996.
At least by his standards.
Other batsmen
would have been proud of his scores.

There were several problems.
One was a knee injury.
It was only a little injury,
but it never seemed to go away.
So Brian was never quite at his best.

Also the West Indian team
was beginning to fall apart.

They had a bad series against Australia.
Several players did not play well.
Brian did not play well.
He thought the players were too wild.
They needed discipline.

He said so loudly,
and that got him branded a trouble-maker.
He was even fined and suspended.

That didn't help his cricket.

In fact the Australians
think they've got Brian sussed.
They think they know where his weaknesses are.
They think they can get him out easily.

They are wrong!

Now Brian is keener than ever
to prove himself again.
He wants to show those records weren't flukes.
He is fit again,
and hungry for runs.

And the team is getting itself
back together again.
So remember what he said
about West Indians.
They want to score fours off every ball.
Well, Brian might not score them
on every ball,
but you can be sure
this quiet young man from Trinidad
with the big smile,
will be scoring fours
for many years yet.